Richard Nixon: A Short Biography
37th President of the United States

Table of Contents

Preface

Welcome to the book, *Richard Nixon: A Short Biography*. This book is part of the 30 Minute Book Series and, as the name of the series implies, if you are an average reader this book will take around 30 minutes to read. Since this short book is not meant to be an all-encompassing biography of Richard Nixon, you may want to know more about this man and his accomplishments. To help you with this, there are several good references at the end of this book. Thank you for purchasing this book. I hope you enjoy your time reading about former President Nixon.

Doug West
June 2017

Introduction

"It takes many good deeds to build a good reputation, and only one bad one to lose it." - Benjamin Franklin

The legacy of Richard M. Nixon, the 37th President of the United States, has been tainted by the long shadow of the Watergate Scandal that has colored history's view of this past president and his accomplishments. Without that large black spot on his record, we might be looking back and calling him a president with great accomplishments — as he was.

Nixon succeeded in opening the Western world to the vast and isolated country of China. He achieved détente with the Soviet Union, which laid the ground work for strategic arm limitation treaties. In the always challenging region of the Middle East, he moved Egypt from the sphere of Soviet influence, strengthened America's ties with the two key allies of Jordan and Saudi Arabia, and helped save Israel in the 1973 Yom Kippur War.

His accomplishments weren't limited to foreign policy. Nixon entered the White House in an era of great turmoil on the home front. The civil rights movement was in full bloom, America was embroiled in the sticky and messy war in Vietnam, and protesters filled the streets of many large cities and the halls of premier universities. Under Nixon's direction, the government extended a helping hand to large groups of minorities. He achieved the peaceful desegregation of Southern schools in 1971 and continued the integration of Northern unions. Native Americans benefited under Nixon by ending the policy of assimilation, which paid Indians to give up their treaty rights and relocate to inner cities. He vastly increased the number of women appointed to senior government positions and ended funding discrimination in college sports by signing Title IX legislation. The draft ended under Nixon and he gave eighteen-year-olds the right to vote. The environment fared well during the Nixon administration with the creation of the Environmental Protection Agency and the National Oceanic and Atmospheric Administration, and Nixon signed both the Clean Air and Clean Water Acts. This enviable record of accomplishment was made even though Congress was controlled by the opposite party.

And then there was the Watergate Scandal and a thousand good deeds became shrouded in the fog of history and contempt of the American conscience. Read on and learn the story of this complex man and his rise and fall from grace.

Chapter 1 – Early Life

"People react to fear, not love; they don't teach that in Sunday School, but it's true." - Richard M. Nixon

Richard Milhous Nixon was born in Yorba Linda, California, a small agricultural community 35 miles east of Los Angeles, on January 9, 1913. He was the son of Francis Anthony and Hannah Milhous Nixon, a couple belonging to the Quaker religious sect known as the Society of Friends. His upbringing was influenced by the evangelical Quaker faith of his parents, which promoted a puritan lifestyle where alcohol, dancing, and swearing were prohibited. The family struggled financially and their lives were marked by hardship. Frank had a small lemon grove business which eventually failed, and he was forced to take odd jobs to support his wife and five sons. Hannah was a very compassionate and calm woman, in startling contrast to her husband, but the couple had a solid relationship.

In 1922, the family moved to Whittier, California, Hannah's birthplace, where the bustling life of the town promised more opportunities for work. Shortly after moving, Frank opened a gas station and later expanded it to include a grocery store. The success of the new enterprise provided the family with the possibility to lead a comfortable middle-class life for a while, even though they still went through different crises from time to time. Richard had a close relationship with his father, learning from Frank that determination and drive meant success. Frank was also passionately interested in politics, always arguing against the Democrats. He taught Richard not only that power was important but also that power was strictly linked with fear, as Frank himself was feared in his family.

Richard was very intelligent and had an uncanny ability to memorize anything along with a deep curiosity for the world around him. During his years at Whittier High School, Nixon devoted long hours daily to his parents' business, working both at the gas station and at the grocery store. He played football with little success as his small frame kept him on the bench most of the time, yet his qualities were able to shine best when he became interested in debating and won a series of championships. Despite the many hours he worked for the family business, he managed to graduate third in his class. For his excellent academic merits, Nixon was offered a scholarship to study at Harvard University, but the financial difficulties of his family forced him to stay at home, where his help was needed at the store. Moreover, one of his brothers suffered from tuberculosis and Nixon had to help his mother take care of his siblings.

Figure – Richard Nixon's high school yearbook picture

Nixon stayed in his hometown and enrolled at Whittier College, a Quaker institution. Still working at his father's store, he found the time to engage in the extracurricular activities of the campus. In his freshman year, he was elected president of his class, president of his fraternity, and president of the History Club. He liked to try everything, from entering debate contests or acting in plays, to trying out for football and basketball. Despite his popularity and active lifestyle, he had few close friends and struggled with personal relationships. Academically, he was an excellent student. While still at Whittier, he met Ola Florence Welch, daughter of the town's police chief. The couple got engaged in 1933 but broke up two years later.

In 1934, after graduating with a B.A. in history, Nixon earned a scholarship to attend Duke Law School. He spent three years at the law school, during which his lack of financial means made him adopt a spartan existence. Since he could not afford his own room, he struggled with living accommodations, finally managing to find an abandoned tool shack at the periphery of the campus, where he lived for a while. Even though he was elected President of the Duke Student Bar Association, Nixon never socialized much and was often characterized as withdrawn and aloof. He worked long hours at the library and spent most of his time studying.

The Duke University School of Law offered generous scholarships to top students, and many professors were high-profile personalities, many of them internationally known. Despite the fierce competition between students, Nixon kept his scholarship and graduated third in his class.

His excellent academic record gave Nixon hopes that he could join the Federal Bureau of Investigation. Due to budget cuts, his letter of application did not bring him the desired outcome. In 1937, since he was unable to find employment in New York, he returned to Whittier to practice law in his hometown. He found a job in commercial litigation for a local law firm and after gaining some experience, he became a full partner in the firm.

In January 1938, shortly after his return to Whittier, Nixon started to date Thelma "Pat" Ryan, a high school teacher. Like Nixon, Pat had grown up without wealth or privilege, born in a miner's shack in Nevada. The couple met during a play rehearsal and after two years of courtship, Ryan accepted Nixon's marriage proposal.

They were married on June 21, 1940, and would later have two daughters, Tricia and Julie.

Pat encouraged her husband's professional ambitions. As both of them believed that Whittier did not offer Nixon many prospects for developing his career, the couple moved to Washington, D.C., in January 1942. Nixon gave up the law practice and started to work for the Office of Price Administration. The escalation of World War II forced him to change paths just four months after coming to Washington, as he decided to join the U.S. Navy.

He was assigned to the Naval Air Station in Ottumwa, Iowa, where he remained until May 1943. After being promoted to lieutenant, Nixon requested sea duty. For his work in the Navy, he received letters of recommendation from commanding officers who praised him for his meritorious service, efficiency, and devotion to duty. In October 1945, he became lieutenant commander. After the war had drawn to a close in 1946, he was released from duty and resigned his commission. He left the military with the rank of lieutenant commander after four years of service mostly on South Pacific islands. He remained in the U.S. Naval Reserve until June 1966.

Chapter 2 – Rising Political Star

"Never say no when a client asks for something, even if it is the moon. You can always try, and anyhow there is plenty of time afterwards to explain that it was not possible." - Richard M. Nixon

In 1945, in California's 12th congressional district, the Republicans were frustrated by their inability to win the seat to Congress. As they sought a candidate who could run a strong and successful campaign, a banker from Whittier recommended Richard Nixon, whom he had known for a long time. Nixon accepted the offer enthusiastically as he was waiting for his discharge from the Navy in Baltimore, Maryland, and this marked the beginning of his political career. As soon as his obligations in the Navy were complete, Nixon and his wife returned to Whittier, where he started to run an intensive campaign.

Excited by the new prospects, Nixon developed an effective campaigning strategy. By stating his support for individual freedom and individual initiative, Nixon appealed to the interests of the small businessmen and farmers who were against labor unions and disliked Democratic policies. Despite his reserved and slightly awkward demeanor, he was skilled at making speeches in which he tenaciously attacked his opponents. Taking advantage of the country's paranoid fear of communism, which was a consequence of the Cold War between the United States and the Soviet Union, Nixon decided to build for himself the reputation of an anti-communist crusader. As many other Republicans who won office during the '40s and '50s, Nixon accused his opponent of being a communist sympathizer to undermine his credibility, even though he was aware of how untrue the accusation was. The habit of accusing his opponents of being hidden communists or communist sympathizers would become his most common campaign practice for many of the elections of his career. To the satisfaction of the Californian Republicans, Nixon won the race to Congress.

Figure - Election poster distributed on behalf of Richard Nixon's campaign for Congress, 1946

As a new congressman, Nixon didn't face many difficulties. Not only was he a fast learner, he was also highly interested in growing his influence. Shortly after the election, he became involved in several high-profile projects, such as the Taft-Hartley Act of 1947, which imposed restrictions on union activities and demanded that union leaders take loyalty oaths. He actively supported the Marshall Plan, a program of financial support aimed toward the reconstruction of Europe after the devastating effects of World War II.

During his early years in politics, Nixon was also a member of the House of Un-American Activities Committee, an official organization that had the role of investigating and exposing within the American society individuals and organizations with communist sympathies which might conspire against the government. From this position, Nixon launched an investigation of Alger Hiss, a former official in the State Department suspected of communist affiliations. Although Hiss denied any charges, he was convicted in 1950 for perjury and espionage operations for the Soviet Union, after the investigators revealed incriminating documents. As the Hiss case received a lot of public attention, Nixon benefited from the publicity as well. His role in exposing the case transformed him into a national figure in the anti-communist battle.

After two terms in Congress, Nixon decided to run for a Senate seat in 1950. Following his typical campaign tactic, he undermined his opponent, Helen Gahagan Douglas, through accusations of being soft on communism. Since the fear of communists had increased dramatically during that time in the United States, the accusations were severe, yet not uncommon. Many Americans were accused of being communists simply because they preferred different lifestyles or held different opinions or values than the politicians themselves. It was during this campaign that Nixon would get the nickname "Tricky Dick," which would stick with him for decades.

In the Senate, Nixon established himself as an anti-communism advocate and he assumed the task of traveling to developing countries to speak out against the threat of global communism. He was not reluctant to criticize President Harry S. Truman for his ineffective handling of the Korean War. His attack on the president suggested that losing the war in Korea was an unpardonable mistake. When it came to domestic issues, Nixon supported civil rights for minorities but voted against price controls, public power, and benefits for illegal immigrants.

Chapter 3 – Vice President of the United States

"Never let your head hang down. Never give up and sit down and grieve. Find another way. And don't pray when it rains if you don't pray when the sun shines." - Richard M. Nixon

While in the Senate, Nixon focused his attention on working toward a higher office. Despite his somewhat confrontational nature, his political career developed quickly. In 1952, he was chosen as Dwight Eisenhower's running mate in the presidential election since Eisenhower wanted a young vice president who could attract the support of the conservative Republicans. Although he was only 39 years old when he was nominated, Nixon had a remarkable reputation and the fact that he was based in California, one of the largest states, was beneficial to Eisenhower's campaign.

However, this remarkable achievement was plagued by a scandal when several newspapers revealed that as a senator, Nixon established a hidden fund where he gathered donations from California businessmen who expected political favors in return. The Republicans strongly advised Eisenhower to remove Nixon from the race, claiming that he would ruin the campaign. While Eisenhower was already considering eliminating him from the campaign, Nixon reacted promptly with a televised speech in which he fully disclosed his personal finances to restore his credibility. He denied any charges of corruption, claiming that he had never received political gifts. To gain sympathy, he talked about his wife and his daughters, confessing that the only gift he did receive was a little cocker spaniel dog named "Checkers" for his six-year-old daughter Tricia. Using a heavy emotional tactic, Nixon portrayed himself and his family as people of modest means. The speech, which became known as the "Checkers" speech, had an audience of almost 60 million people and launched a massive outpouring of support for Nixon, saving his career and allowing him to maintain his position in the race.

As the campaign continued, Eisenhower proved to be a calm and laid-back personality, whose idea of a campaign was very different from that of Nixon, who was more aggressive. Eisenhower spoke of optimistic plans for the future while Nixon assumed a negative stance focusing on undermining their opponents through continuous attacks. As usual, Nixon appealed to his unbeatable strategy, and he accused the Democratic nominee and Illinois governor Adlai Stevenson of being soft on communism. Unsurprisingly, the Eisenhower and Nixon ticket won the election and assumed the presidency.

In 1953, Nixon became the vice president of the United States. Eisenhower gave Nixon a more active role as vice president than was typical for the position. Nixon attended Cabinet and National Security Council meetings and chaired the meetings during Eisenhower's absences. Since Eisenhower's health was very frail and he went through three major illnesses during his presidency, Nixon had the opportunity to enforce his position more than was usually normal for his office. Although Eisenhower was a popular president, when his health issues impeded him from running the office as he would have liked, Nixon stepped in. The most severe crisis was in 1955 when Eisenhower suffered a heart attack and was out of service for six weeks, during which Nixon had to take over the Oval Office and take care of administrative issues. Nixon's biographer, Steven Ambrose, reported on the period that Nixon had "earned the high praise he received for his conduct during the crisis…He made no attempt to seize power."

Nixon was regarded as the first truly modern vice president because of his willingness to maintain an intimate collaboration between his office and that of the president. He encouraged presidential initiatives and devoted a lot of energy to accomplish the goals of the White House. During this time, his influence within the Republican wing of the Congress grew significantly, especially because he positioned himself against several of Eisenhower's policies when he felt it necessary.

Even though most Republicans were afraid that health problems made Eisenhower unfit for a second term as president, he managed to make a full recovery and in early 1956, he announced his second candidacy. Despite Nixon's efforts to maintain his position, his career faced a serious threat when several advisors of Eisenhower suggested that the president to choose a new running mate for the 1956 presidential election. Eisenhower tried to convince Nixon to not seek a new nomination and offered him another position in the Cabinet. Nixon refused and Eisenhower decided to keep him as his running mate. Eisenhower and Nixon were reelected by a sizable margin in the November 1956 election.

The most memorable visit was the 1959 tour of the Soviet Union when he met Soviet Premier Nikita Khrushchev and engaged in a controversial debate about the differences between the capitalist and socialist governments. Nixon managed to make a good impression during the so-called "kitchen debate," where he subtly proclaimed the superiority of the American society over the Soviet model. By defending the capitalist society and exposing the weaknesses of communism, Nixon emerged as the emblematic anti-communist figure.

Nixon was very successful in handling the majority of issues and traveled frequently to countries of Europe, Asia, and Africa as a goodwill ambassador of the United States. While he was mostly well received in most places, this was not the case for South America, where a more violent protest occurred.

Chapter 4 – The Election of 1960 and the "Wilderness" Years

"You won't have Nixon to kick around anymore, because, gentlemen, this is my last press conference." - Richard M. Nixon

In 1960, as a result of his growing influence, Nixon was nominated as the Republican candidate for the presidential election. He emerged as a frontrunner in the initial phases, but the campaign proved to be tough, as Nixon had to run against the more popular Democratic nominee, John F. Kennedy. Kennedy was the opposite of Nixon; he was movie-star handsome, with an equally beautiful wife. Born into wealth, he was the son of one of the richest men in America with strong ties to the eastern establishment. Nixon and Kennedy weren't from the same class. Nixon had no wealth or family connections to rely on; he had ascended to the position of vice president on his own through hard work, grit, and determination.

After winning the primaries, Nixon received the Republican nomination quite early compared to Kennedy, who struggled to lock up the Democratic nomination. With his extensive campaign experience and vigorous temperament, Nixon established a strong, overwhelming lead in the rating polls. However, this changed promptly after a series of televised debates between the two candidates. It was the first time that a presidential campaign debate was broadcast on television since television had only recently become common in most American households.

Figure - John F. Kennedy and Richard Nixon, taken prior to their first debate in Chicago in 1960

During the debates, Kennedy offered to the public a positive image of himself, appearing as a lively and optimistic idealist with a relaxed and pleasant demeanor. Nixon, on the contrary, seemed rather tired, with an unkempt look and a boring program of almost no interesting plans for the future. Moreover, he couldn't use his old strategy of accusing his opponent of communist sympathies, as Kennedy was a well-known anti-communist. Despite the obvious differences between the two candidates, the debate did not help either of them to gain a solid advantage in the polls. Even though some analysts argued that Nixon's points had been more poignant during the debates, Kennedy managed to swing the odds in his favor during the final weeks of the campaign. Moreover, when asked to give his opinion on Nixon, Eisenhower commented in a way that suggested Nixon had been incompetent as his vice president, which put Nixon into an uncomfortable position again. Eventually, Nixon lost by less than one percent in the popular vote while he only managed to get 220 to Kennedy's 303 votes in the Electoral College. Disappointed by the result, Nixon had no other choice than to return to California, yet he did not give up his political ambitions but rather decided to shift his focus elsewhere.

After losing the election to Kennedy and ending his term as vice president, Nixon resumed his work as an attorney and spent his spare time writing a book on his former political activities, such as the Hiss case, and Eisenhower's heart attack, among others. The book, entitled *Six Crises*, rapidly became a bestseller. In 1962, Nixon made an unexpected comeback as he decided to run for California's gubernatorial seat. At first, he was reluctant to enter the race, and his campaign suffered because of a general suspicion that he viewed the office only as a step toward a second presidential run. As the campaign progressed, Nixon hoped that a victory would establish him as a leading Republican on the national scene. He returned to his old practices during the campaign, maintaining an aggressive stance against his opponent and accusing him of hiding communist sympathies. However, his strategy failed and the Democrat nominee Edmund G. Brown won the race by more than five percent. With one more disappointment on his record, Nixon turned into a defensive mode, blaming the press for unfair treatment. Nixon felt he had received unfair coverage from the media, saying, "You won't have Nixon to kick around anymore." Many believed that this crushing defeat would keep him away from politics.

In 1963, after the election, Nixon and his family went on an extensive trip to Europe, where Nixon met the political leaders of the countries they visited and gave press conferences. Upon their return to the U.S., the family moved to New York City. Once again, Nixon found himself forced to return to law practice. The last failure convinced him to let go of his political ambitions, at least temporarily. He became a senior partner in a leading law firm.

In New York, Nixon discovered that his defeat was not necessarily the end of his political career. He immersed himself again in politics, as he started to campaign for the Republican Party all over the country. Slowly, but steadily, he made his great comeback. When Nixon revealed to his family that he planned to run for president again, his wife showed him her support, despite the fact that she had not enjoyed the attention brought by a public life.

Chapter 5 – President of the United States

"I wish I could give you a lot of advice, based on my experience of winning political debates. But I don't have that experience. My only experience is at losing them." - Richard M. Nixon

When the 1968 presidential nomination approached, Nixon was already regarded as the most reasonable option, since he was a moderate candidate among names such as California's governor Ronald Reagan, or New York's governor Nelson Rockefeller. The race to the nomination was one of the easiest that Nixon ever entered. In his speech as the Republican nominee for the presidential election of 1968, Nixon shared his strong belief in the American dream and his conviction that the United States would leave behind its darkest days, reaching for greatness again. Nixon chose Maryland Governor Spiro Agnew as his running mate. Nixon's strategy was that with Agnew on the ticket, this would unite the party, appealing to both Northern moderates and disillusioned Southern Democrats.

During the party's convention in Miami, demonstrators gathered outside the convention hall to protest the Vietnam War, which led to a series of confrontations that would mark a period of great unrest throughout the United States. Political and social issues such as the Vietnam War and civil rights led to massive protests and acts of violence, including the assassination of civil rights leader Martin Luther King, Jr., and former U.S. attorney general Robert F. Kennedy, who had been one of the potential Democratic presidential nominees. Eventually, the Democrats nominated Vice President Hubert Humphrey.

Having the experience of a past presidential campaign, Nixon developed a better and more efficient strategy the second time. His campaign was based on the need for law and order that had become an imperative in American society. He directed his speeches toward what he called the "forgotten Americans," referring to people who work hard and respect their government. The campaign was a real challenge, as Nixon had to convince voters that he could be trusted and provide answers for the crises in American society, such as the racial issues, Vietnam War, and class struggles. Nixon decided to appeal mostly to the white middle class and tried to strategically position himself as more responsible and competent than his opponent, Hubert Humphrey. By portraying himself as a campion for security and stability in the face of the unsettling national unrest, Nixon gathered the support of the socially conservative Americans for whom the counterculture with its hippies and protesters represented a threat. Nixon's running mate, Spiro Agnew, became the most vocal detractor of the countercultural groups to secure Nixon's influence over the right wing.

Figure – Richard Nixon gives his trademark "victory" during his successful 1968 campaign to become President of the United States

Nixon promised to maintain open and honest relations with the press and the public. While he was working to restore his former influence, Agnew provoked a few incidents that almost ruined their campaign. He made outrageous declarations to the press in which he openly discriminated against people based on racial and social motives.

Nixon's basic campaign promise was twofold: He would end the war in Vietnam and restore law and order to the country. By 1968, the country was rapidly swirling toward anarchy with the assassination of Martin Luther King, Jr., and Robert Kennedy; there had been violent riots in at least nineteen cities; and some of the largest universities had been brought to their knees by student sit-ins and protests. Apparently, the American voters liked what they saw and heard from Nixon as he won the popular vote over Herbert Humphrey by a single percentage point (43.43 percent to Humphrey's 42.72 percent), with the third-party candidate, George Wallace, capturing less than fourteen percent. Nixon's victory was the end of the New Deal coalition first assembled by Franklin Roosevelt, and he was the first president since Zachary Taylor whose party did not control either house of Congress.

Nixon was sworn in as the 37th President on January 20, 1969. By the time he took office, the domestic unrest in American society increased. Citizens were protesting not only for the end of the Vietnam War, but also for environmental protection, civil rights for women and minorities, and other social causes. After a massive oil spill incident in Santa Barbara, California, Nixon pushed for a law that set the foundation for the Environmental Protection Agency, which took the task of regulating environmental issues. He also signed the Clean Air Act and the Endangered Species Act.

Along with his progressive attitude toward the environmental cause, Nixon preserved a moderate conservative stance when it came to civil rights. As Nixon appointed four Supreme Court justices known for their conservative views, any change seemed impossible. However, during his time in office, the federal government pushed for the desegregation of many public schools and special funding was set aside for the enforcement of civil rights. Nixon supported the Equal Rights Amendment meant to eliminate sex discrimination, and he appointed a White House adviser to cover women's issues.

A common reproach that Nixon received for his presidency was that he increased spending in national defense while reducing the funds for education and antipoverty programs in his attempts to keep government spending under control. During his presidency, Nixon had to deal with an economy weakened by inflation, which convinced him to initiate and promote programs meant to lower U.S. imports while increasing exports.

The major economic goal of Nixon's presidency was thus to reduce the staggering high inflation. Aware that one of the causes of inflation was the war, and that the cause could not be eliminated promptly, Nixon focused on other means. When Congress granted Nixon the authority to impose wage and price controls, most congressmen believed he would be reluctant to launch the policy, since he had previously opposed such measures throughout his career. However, to secure votes in the possibility of a re-election by convincing Americans that he was interested in their financial wellbeing, Nixon agreed to the measure. By 1972, inflation had dropped, but Nixon's decision to devalue the dollar in an attempt to keep inflation low led to the opposite effect.

Regarding domestic issues, Nixon decided to delegate some of his minor responsibilities to other members of his administration. While Nixon and Henry Kissinger focused on the pressing foreign issues, his aides, chief of staff H.R. Haldeman and campaign advisor John Ehrilchman, dealt with local issues. Henry Kissinger worked closely with Nixon on matters relating to foreign affairs, serving as the National Security advisor, and also as Secretary of State from 1973 to 1977. By all appearances, Nixon succeeded at enforcing important policies, yet he struggled to collaborate with Kissinger, whom he thought to be treacherous and power-hungry.

***

After a relatively successful first term in office, the Nixon-Agnew team was unanimously nominated as the Republican contender for the 1972 presidential election. The hopes of Democrats for regaining the White House were buoyed by congressional victories in the mid-term elections. The Democrats chose South Dakota Senator George McGovern, who, in turn, selected liberal Senator Thomas Eagleton of Missouri as his running mate.

Nixon portrayed himself as the responsible and moderate candidate representing the "silent majority," a candidate who would end the war and reject "the far out goals of the far left." The Democrats ran into trouble when it was revealed that Eagleton had undergone shock treatments for depression years earlier. McGovern quickly forced Eagleton from the ticket and replaced him with a little-known Kennedy clan member and former director of the War on Poverty, Sargent Shriver.

On election day, Nixon carried the vote, winning forty-nine of the fifty states in a landslide victory. Despite the fact that 18-to-21-year-olds could now vote, turnout at the polls was the lowest it had been in decades. Democrats retained control of Congress, indicating that voters were not as much turned on by Nixon as they were turned off by McGovern.

Chapter 6 – The Vietnam War and Foreign Relations

"No event in American history is more misunderstood than the Vietnam War. It was misreported then, and it is misremembered now." - Richard M. Nixon

In the early 1950s, an uprising in a French colony in southeast Asia, French Indochina, led the French to abandon the area, which would be divided into four new nations based on historical boundaries— Cambodia, Laos, and North and South Vietnam. Later in that same decade, North Vietnamese communist solders called the Vietcong invaded South Vietnam with the intention of overthrowing the existing government and replacing it with a communist system of government. America had been supporting the South Vietnamese with shipments of supplies and military advisors during the Eisenhower and Kennedy administrations. American involvement in the war escalated in 1965 under President Lyndon Johnson, with bombing missions against the Vietcong. By the end of the year, American combat troops began arriving and by 1968, there would be a half million Americans on Vietnam's soil.

When Nixon took office in 1969, his goal was achieving "peace with honor," and he began a program of withdrawing troops. By August, 25,000 troops had left Vietnam and by December another 65,000 were shipped back to the States. Nixon wanted to implement a policy of "Vietnamization" or training and equipping the South Vietnamese soldier to fight. Despite Nixon's plans, the war kept expanding. In 1970, American air and ground forces crossed into the neighboring neutral country of Cambodia to destroy Vietcong strongholds. The following year, American B-52 bombers started hitting targets in the country of Laos to destroy Vietcong supply lines along the Ho Chi Minh trail. In March 1972, American bombers began an assault on North Vietnam and later that year mines were placed in northern harbors to disrupt arms shipments from the Soviet Union. With the breakdown of peace talks in 1972, Nixon escalated bombing of the north, which would become the largest aerial bombing up until that point.

Figure – Map of Vietnam Region 1966-1967

A ceasefire was agreed upon in January 1973, and by 1974 all American personnel were evacuated from Vietnam. Direct U.S. military involvement ended in

August of 1973. The capture of the South Vietnamese capitol city of Saigon by the North Vietnamese army in April 1975 marked the end of the war, with North and South Vietnam reunified the following year. With America's involvement in the war over, the death toll of American soldiers stood at over 60,000 dead or missing in action with more than 150,000 wounded.

***

Despite his aggressive policies in Southeast Asia, foreign policy was the area where Richard Nixon had the most impressive accomplishments of his political career. In 1972, he made a historic trip to communist China, despite the long years of heavy criticism and attacks on communism. In July 1971, Nixon announced his upcoming visit to China on both television and radio. The news was astonishing for the world, yet Nixon and the Beijing leaders had been preparing for the visit for nearly a year to make sure that the political climate of their countries would support the contact. The meeting between the American president and the Chinese government was the first high-level contact between the two nations in over twenty years, and it established strategic commitments and a trade agreement. As part of the visit to China, Nixon toured the Forbidden City, Ming Tombs, and the Great Wall. While her husband was in meetings, Pat Nixon, accompanied by a television crew, toured the city of Beijing, and visited schools, factories, and hospitals. The visit led the way for a new era of Sino-American relations and pressured the Soviets for détente with America.

In the same year, Nixon also visited the Soviet Union with the purpose of launching a policy of détente in an attempt to reduce the tensions between the two countries and to promote diplomatic and commercial connections. The president and first lady arrived in Moscow on May 22, 1972, and met with General Secretary of the Communist Party, Leonid Brezhnev, and top Soviet officials. Nixon signed a new trade agreement with Soviet leader Brezhnev and proposed a missile reduction program, the Strategic Arms Limitation Treaty (SALT). To give the Soviets proof of his good intentions, he allowed the sale of a massive quantity of American wheat to the Soviets, who had suffered a shortage after the implementation of some disastrous agricultural programs. As a result of the meetings and agreements, Nixon and Brezhnev claimed a new era of "peaceful coexistence."

Chapter 7 – Watergate Scandal

"You must pursue this investigation of Watergate even if it leads to the president. I'm innocent. You've got to believe I'm innocent. If you don't, take my job." - Richard M. Nixon

The incident that triggered the scandal that forced a sitting president from office started with a burglary at the Democratic National Committee headquarters at the Watergate office complex in Washington, D.C., on June 17, 1972. By investigating the burglary and arresting the burglars, the FBI discovered a connection between the five burglars and the Committee for the Re-Election of the President (CPR, but better known as CREEP), which was the official organization of Nixon's campaign. In January 1972, the Finance Counsel for CREEP, G. Gordon Mitchell, CREEP's Acting Chairman Jeb Stuart Magruder, Attorney General John Mitchell, and Presidential Counsel John Dean planned an extensive illegal operation against the Democratic Party. Their plan was to enter the Democratic National Committee's (DNC) headquarters at the Watergate Complex in Washington, D.C., for burglary and installing listening devices in the telephones. Liddy was designated the leader of the operation. Two former CIA officers, Edward Hunt and James McCord, were also involved. They broke in to the DNC's headquarters on May 28 and managed to wiretap two phones inside the offices. Even though the CREEP agents successfully installed the listening devices, they later discovered that the devices needed repair and they planned a second break-in to fix the issues.

Figure - Watergate Complex in Washington, D.C.

In the early morning hours of June 17, 1972, one of the security guards at the Watergate Complex noticed strange movements inside the offices and alerted the police. McCord and four Cuban men were found inside the DNC's headquarters. They were arrested and charged with attempted burglary and attempted interception of telephone and other communications. In January 1973, they were convicted of burglary, violation of federal wiretapping laws, and conspiracy. During the investigation of the burglary, Nixon's organization quickly started to plan a cover up that would remove any harmful evidence against the president. Several officials of the Nixon administration were afraid that Hunt and Liddy would have all their activities scrutinized since they were also part of a separate secret operation that was concerned with stopping leaks and managing sensitive security matters.

When informed about the break-in, Nixon proved to be slightly skeptical about the affair, yet he started to worry. As revealed by the tape of a June 23, 1972, conversation between Nixon and White House Chief of Staff H.R. Haldeman, the president did not have any knowledge of the burglary, but he was directly involved in the attempts to cover up the incident. During the conversation, Nixon expressed his intention of pressuring the FBI and CIA to stop the investigations into the Watergate case under the pretense that national security secrets could be exposed if the FBI would inquire into the events in greater depth.

Nixon officially stated that no one in the White House or his administration had any part in the strange incident. However, examinations of the burglars' bank accounts showed there was a close link between them and the finance committee of CREEP. They had received thousands of dollars in checks earmarked for Nixon's re-election campaign. Despite their attempts to cover up the origins of the money, the FBI investigation revealed records of the transactions. Soon, the FBI found several direct and indirect ties between the burglars and CREEP, causing suspicion that government officials were also involved. On October 10, 1972, the FBI's reports exposed the connection between the Watergate break-in and a massive campaign of political espionage and sabotage against the Democrats on behalf of Nixon's re-election committee.

Despite these public revelations, Nixon's presidential campaign did not suffer. In November, he was re-elected president. The media, however, was not willing to move on so easily. Investigative coverage by publications such as *Time Magazine*, *The New York Times*, and the *Washington Post* repeatedly highlighted the connection between the Watergate incident and the re-election committee. The media involvement led to a dramatic increase of publicity, which determined political repercussions. Reporters from the *Washington Post* suggested that the entire affair of the break-in and the cover up was linked to the upper branches of the FBI, CIA, the Justice Department, and most surprisingly, the White House. They had an anonymous source, known as "Deep Throat," which was only identified in 2005. He was William Mark Felt, who worked as the deputy director of the FBI during the 1970s. The reporters, Bob Woodward and Carl Bernstein, met Felt secretly several times and found that the White House staff were very concerned with what the Watergate investigations might reveal. Felt was also responsible for anonymous leaks to *Time Magazine* and *Washington Daily News*.

Despite receiving all kinds of information from different sources, the media did not realize the massive implications of the scandal, and everyone focused on the 1972 presidential election. As the trials of the burglars proceeded, the media shifted its attention completely toward the scandal, especially since there was a profound level of distrust between the press and the Nixon administration. For Nixon, it was evident that there was a clash between his administration and the press. He wanted to sanction the hostile media organizations by using the authority of the government agencies, which was something he had previously done. In 1969, the FBI wiretapped the phones of five reporters at Nixon's request and in 1971, the White House explicitly asked for an audit of the tax return of a journalist from *Newsday* who had written articles about the financial operations of Nixon's friend, Charles Rebozo.

To undermine the credibility of the press, the administration and its supporters resorted to accusations, claiming that the media was liberal and thus had a bias against the Republican administration. Despite the accusations, the media coverage on the Watergate scandal proved accurate. Moreover, the competition typical of the media ensured wide and extensive investigations from different angles.

While many expected the Watergate case to end with the conviction of the five burglars in January 1973, the investigations continued and the evidence against Nixon and his administration grew. To remove threats of incrimination, Nixon put forth a new cover up operation. The relationships between Nixon, his close aides, and other directly involved officials grew tense, as accusations were made from each side. On April 30, Nixon demanded the resignation of several of his aides, including Attorney General Kleindienst and White House Counsel John Dean. This prompted the United States Senate to establish a committee in charge of the Watergate investigation. The hearings of the Senate Committee were broadcast and the live covering of the hearings ran from May 17 to August 7, 1973. The estimations suggest that 85% of Americans watched at least portions of the hearings.

By July 1973, the evidence against the president's staff mounted, especially after the Senate Watergate Committee obtained testimony from Nixon's former staff members. Forced to give a testimony before the Senate Watergate Committee, White House assistant Alexander Butterfield confessed that the conversations in the Oval

Office, the Cabinet Room, one of Nixon's private offices, and other places were secretly taped by devices that automatically recorded everything. The information was of extraordinary importance for the investigations because it had the power to transform the entire course of events. Unsurprisingly, the new information led to a series of fierce court battles in which the president tried to keep the tapes hidden. The Senate requested Nixon release the tapes, yet he refused, using as an excuse his executive privileges as president. Since the official prosecutor also refused to drop his request, Nixon demanded the attorney general and his deputy fire him. Both men refused to follow the order and resigned in protest. Nixon did not stop here. Eventually, Solicitor General Robert Bork complied with Nixon's order and dismissed the prosecutor. While accomplishing his goal, Nixon discovered that his actions were heavily condemned by the public. On November 17, 1973, he spoke before 400 Associated Press managing editors to explain his decisions after accusations of wrongdoing. The Watergate investigation passed under the charge of new special prosecutor Leon Jaworksi.

On March 1, 1974, seven former aides of Nixon, later known as the "Watergate Seven," were indicted by the grand jury for conspiracy in hindering the Watergate investigation. President Nixon was named secretly unindicted co-conspirator. A month later, Nixon's former appointment's secretary was convicted of perjury before the Senate Committee. Nixon had to decide which recorded materials could be safely released to the public. His advisers argued about whether the recordings should be edited to remove profanity and vulgarity. They eventually released an edited version after several debates.

In a public speech held on April 29, 1974, Nixon made an official announcement about the release of the transcripts. The reactions to the speech were positive, yet as more people read the transcripts over the following weeks, there was a wave of indignation among the public and the media. Former supporters of Nixon now asked for his resignation or impeachment. As a direct consequence, Nixon's reputation deteriorated quickly and irreversibly. Even though the transcripts did not reveal criminal offenses, they showed a deplorable side of Nixon's personality and his contempt for the United States and its institutions, as proved by the vindictive tone and vulgar language of the conversations.

On July 24, 1974, the U.S. Supreme Court decided unanimously that executive privilege did not extend over the tapes in the United States v. Nixon trial regarding the access to the tapes. The president had the legal obligation to allow government investigators access to the tapes. With no possibility of escaping the decision of the court, Nixon complied. The court ordered Nixon to release all the tapes to the special prosecutor. The tapes were made public on July 30, 1974, revealing crucial information. The entire cover up operations in the Watergate case were exposed through the recorded conversations between the president and his counsel, John Dean. Both Nixon and Dean were aware that their actions and those of their aides, including paying the burglary team for their silence, fell under obstruction of justice. The audio recordings revealed extensive conversation between Nixon and his top staff members, in which he spoke openly about his attempts to force the FBI and CIA to cease investigation on the Watergate break-in. The recordings showed that Nixon was not only aware of the payments to the Watergate defendants, but also that he had approved them willingly. Further investigations on the recordings proved that more than 18 minutes of tape had been erased.

On February 6, 1974, the Judiciary Committee received approval to investigate the president for impeachment under articles such as obstruction of justice, abuse of power, and contempt of Congress. The decisive event in the impeachment process was the release of a new tape, which would later become known as the "smoking gun." Released on August 5, 1974, the tape contained a documented description of the cover up operation in all its stages. Nixon had denied for a long time any accusations of being involved in the scandal, but all his lies were fully exposed by the tape, completely destroying his credibility.

Threatened with impeachment by the House of Representatives and with conviction by the Senate, Nixon had to make a decision. On August 8, 1974, realizing that impeachment was certain and he had no chance to keep his office, President Richard Nixon resigned. In his farewell address to the White House staff on that same day, Nixon said:

"...And so I say to you on this occasion, as we leave, we leave proud of the people who have stood by us and worked for us and served this country. We want you to be proud of what you have done. We want you to continue to serve in government, if that is your wish. Always give your best, never get discouraged, never be petty; always remember, others may hate you, but those who hate you don't win unless you hate them, and then you destroy yourself. Thank you very much."

His resignation finally put an end to the Watergate scandal, yet with disastrous results for American democracy and political life. Vice President Gerald Ford was sworn in as the 38th President of the United States shortly after Nixon's departure. The new president told the nation that, "Our long national nightmare is over." The results of the Watergate investigations led to the indictment of 69 people, of which 48 were found guilty. Most of them were top administration officials of the White House.

Figure – Richard Nixon leaving the White House on Marine One shortly before his resignation became effective, August 9, 1974

On September 8, 1974, President Ford gave an unconditional pardon to Richard Nixon for his role in the Watergate scandal. Ford felt the decision was in the best interest of the nation and would put this dark period in American political history in the past. Ford's popularity dropped dramatically after his decision to pardon Nixon and most political observers believe that cost him the 1976 presidential election to the relative unknown governor from Georgia, Jimmy Carter.

Chapter 8 – Final Years

"Certainly in the next 50 years we shall see a woman president, perhaps sooner than you think. A woman can and should be able to do any political job that a man can do." - Richard M. Nixon

After leaving Washington, Nixon and his wife Pat retreated to their home in San Clemente, California. Despite the magnitude of the scandal that led to his resignation, at the end of 1974, Nixon began to consider a comeback, confessing in his diary that he viewed the entire situation as a test of character which he shouldn't fail.

He spent his time working on his memoirs while putting all his efforts into preventing the release of additional Watergate material. As he was writing the book, he became increasingly worried about his financial situation. His expenses had remained high and he also had to pay lawyer fees, and this was a realization that compelled him to seek work again. In just a couple of months, he managed to sign a contract with British talk-show host and producer David Frost for a series of interviews. During the interviews, the two covered several topics about Nixon's presidency, but the most memorable moments covered the Watergate scandal. Nixon admitted that he had disappointed his citizens and he took blame for the whole affair. The interviews became very popular, with an estimated viewership of over 45 million. Not only did Nixon considerably improve his financial situation, the interviews also helped him in the process of rebuilding his reputation.

The newly found financial security allowed him to respond to Mao's personal invitation to China. In February 1976, Nixon entered China for the second time. However, his desire to establish himself again as an important figure on the world's political scene did not go smoothly. In the United Kingdom, American diplomats and ministers of the Callaghan government avoided him while two former prime ministers ignored requests for a meeting. Nixon was welcomed, however, by the Leader of the Opposition, Margaret Thatcher.

Nixon's memoirs, *RN: The Memoirs of Richard Nixon*, appeared in 1978 and rapidly became a bestseller, attracting favorable responses from the critics. In 1979, Nixon was invited to the White House at the request of President Carter's guest, Chinese Vice Premier Deng Xiaoping. In 1979, Nixon visited China for the third time.

In August 1979, Nixon moved to New York City, where he purchased property. After less than two years, he and his wife retreated to Saddle River, New Jersey. During the 1980s, Nixon remained active on the public scene through speaking engagements, writing, travels, and meetings with foreign leaders. To regain respect as an elder statesman, he continued to travel and talk with world leaders. Nixon made several trips to developing countries in the Middle East. In the United States, the media began to talk about a possible rehabilitation for him. Meanwhile, he continued to travel across the world, making a second visit to the Soviet Union in 1986. Upon his return, he provided President Ronald Reagan with a comprehensive document containing his personal advice on foreign policy and his impressions of the encounter with Soviet leader Mikhail Gorbachev. In the same year, *Newsweek* magazine published a story on Nixon entitled

"He's back." When Bill Clinton assumed office, he and his wife Hillary would often seek Nixon's advice on controversial matters, even though Hillary had been a member of the committee that voted for Nixon's impeachment.

In 1990, the inauguration of the private institution Richard Nixon Library and Birthplace in Yorba Linda, California took place in the presence of former presidents Gerald Ford and George H.W. Bush, along with President Reagan. Half a year later, Nixon founded the Nixon Center, a policy think tank and conference center in Washington, which would later be renamed as the Center for the National Interest. During his retirement years, Nixon wrote nine books on politics, mainly in an attempt to clarify his decisions during his presidency and to rehabilitate himself in the eyes of the American public.

***

On June 22, 1993, Nixon's wife Pat died of lung cancer and emphysema. One year later, on April 18, 1994, Nixon suffered a severe stroke while having dinner at his home in New Jersey. He was taken to the hospital, where the doctors managed to stabilize him. Although he was initially responsive, shortly he became unable to move his right arm or leg and he couldn't speak. The brain damage caused a cerebral edema and Nixon went into a coma. He died four days later, with his daughters standing beside him. He was 81 years old.

Nixon's funeral took place in Yorba Linda, California, with four former presidents attending the ceremony, along with President Bill Clinton and other state officials. According to his final wishes, Nixon did not have a full state funeral, yet many wished to pay their respects. Almost 42,000 people passed by his casket before the funeral service.

With the determination that was characteristic of his political career, Nixon managed during his post-presidency years to rebuild his reputation and redeem himself. The news coverage that followed upon his death mentioned Watergate, yet most maintained a favorable attitude toward the former president. However, writer Hunter S. Thompson was less willing to forgive and forget and denounced Nixon in an article for *The Atlantic* entitled "He Was a Crook," in which he called Nixon a political monster.

People who have known Nixon agreed that he had a complex personality, as he was very secretive and reflective, yet slightly awkward, having the unusual habit of distancing himself from people and always maintaining a formal attitude. He was also very driven, showing extreme tenacity and diligence. He would often sabotage himself because of a constant feeling of being misunderstood and underappreciated. Other biographers suggest that he suffered from an uncomfortable shyness despite being an intelligent and talented man. One of his worst flaws was to assume the worst in people, an attitude which finally caused his downfall. His personality was the element that doomed his political career as he was prone to isolation and secrecy. Later in his life, he admitted to feeling paranoid often. His favorite way of communication was writing memoranda, which often expressed violent and aggressive attitudes and constant fear of threats. Despite his promises, he showed that he was driven mostly by his restless pursuit of power, which led him to shake the political foundation of the country, making it succumb to one of its most severe constitutional crises.

Many historians and analysts recognize Nixon's merits in foreign relations, while others still blame him for the disaster he caused in the life of the American democracy. The only conclusion that can be reached is that a verdict is not possible. Most agree, nonetheless, that Nixon had a remarkable role in directing the Republican Party toward a moderate position. He also had a positive influence on the enforcement of crucial environmental and regulatory legislation by creating the Environmental Protection Agency and passing the 1973 Endangered Species Act. His foreign policies, especially regarding the problematic relations with China and the Soviet Union, were practical and sensible. At the same time, many consider his decision to keep the U.S. involved in the Vietnam War inexcusable.

Despite his merits, Nixon left a negative legacy by causing a wave of fundamental mistrust of government that continued to affect the American political scene long after his resignation. As someone who had represented the Republican Party on the national ballot five times, Nixon managed to shake the foundation of the American political scene through his involvement in illegal and undemocratic actions, which overshadowed his remarkable accomplishments in foreign relations and the economy. The institution of the presidency suffered a decrease in power due to Congress imposing restrictive legislation following the Watergate scandal.

Richard Nixon made history in ways that no one expected as he is the only president to resign in the history of the United States. However, the scandal that ensued after

Watergate gave him no choice as otherwise, he would have had to go through a lengthy and embarrassing impeachment trial. Even though he violated the Constitution, broke laws, and lied repeatedly, Nixon's actions were more a symptom of his time, rather than a singular incident in the political life of the United States. By causing the Watergate scandal, Nixon revealed not only his shortcomings but also the decline of ethics in the American political system.

The End

Thank you for reading my book. I hope you found it worth your time and money. Please don't forget to leave a review for this short book. I read each review and they help me become a better writer.
Doug

Timeline

January 9, 1913 - Born in Yorba Linda, California, to Frank and Hannah Milhous Nixon, the second born of five brothers.

1922 - Frank Nixon sells the family home and lemon grove in Yorba Linda, and moves the family to nearby Whittier.

1930 - Richard Nixon finishes third in his high school class, winning numerous awards, including the Harvard Club California award for outstanding all-around student, which earned him a scholarship to Harvard University. Due to the family's limited finances, Nixon forgoes the scholarship and instead attends Whittier College

1934 - At Whittier College Nixon is elected student body president, becomes the founder and elected president of the Orthogonians fraternity, joins the debate team, acts in several plays, and is on the football team.

1937 - Attends Duke University Law School on a scholarship and is a member of the law review. After graduation, he returns to Whittier, where he takes the California bar and is hired by the law firm Wingert and Bewley.

1938 - Meets his future wife, Pat Ryan, at a Whittier Community Players tryout.

June 21, 1940 - Marries Pat Ryan at the Mission Inn in Riverside, California.

1942 - Begins work as an attorney at the Office for Price Administration in Washington, D.C., where he witnesses firsthand the problems of government bureaucracy. The experience greatly influences the policies Nixon later develops during his political career.

August 1942 - Nixon is commissioned as an officer in the U.S. Navy.

January 1944-July 1944 - Nixon receives a battle-station assignment for the South Pacific, first at Bougainville and then at Green Island. While in Bougainville, he opens a "Nick's Hamburger Stand" for flight crews on their way to battle missions.

September 1945 - Nixon is urged by Republican leaders in Whittier to run for a seat in the U.S. House of Representatives.

January 1946 - Nixon is honorably discharged from the U.S. Navy with the rank of lieutenant commander.

February 21, 1946 – The first daughter, Tricia, is born to Richard and Pat Nixon.

November 1946 - Nixon defeats 5-term veteran Democratic Congressman Jerry Voorhis and is elected to represent California's 12th district in the U.S. House of Representatives.

July 5, 1948 – Second daughter, Julie, is born to Richard and Pat Nixon.

1948 - Nixon works as lead committee member in the investigation of accused Soviet spy Alger Hiss, which ultimately uncovers Hiss's role in the Communist Party and conviction on charge of perjury.

1950 - Nixon is elected to the U.S. Senate seat, defeating Democratic congresswoman and one-time Hollywood starlet Helen Gahagan Douglas.

July 11, 1952 - The Republican National Convention ratifies by acclamation Dwight Eisenhower's choice of Richard Nixon as his vice-presidential running mate.

September 23, 1952 - Nixon gives his famous televised Checkers Speech, refuting false charges of fiscal impropriety, retaining his position as vice presidential candidate to General Dwight D. Eisenhower, and gaining nationwide support.

November 4, 1952 - Dwight Eisenhower is elected President of the United States. Senator Nixon is elected as his Vice President.

Spring 1953 - At the request of President Eisenhower, Vice President Nixon—along with Pat Nixon—make a two-month trip to over 30 countries throughout Asia and the Middle East.

September 1955 - President Eisenhower suffers from a heart attack. In his absence, Vice President Nixon presides over regular Cabinet and National Security Council meetings.

July 24, 1959 - Nixon goes head-to-head with Soviet Premier Nikita Khrushchev on the merits of freedom versus communism at the American Exhibition in

Moscow, in what famously becomes known as the "Kitchen Debate."

1960 - Nixon runs for president against Senator John F. Kennedy, participates in the first televised debates, and loses by the smallest popular-vote margin in American history.

1963-1967 "Wilderness Years" - During his years as a private citizen, Vice President Nixon travels across the globe and meets world leaders, and campaigns tirelessly across the country for Republican candidates in the 1964 and 1966 elections.

August 8, 1968 - Nixon is nominated as the Republican candidate for president and pledges to bring the nation together.

November 5, 1968 - Nixon is elected President of the United States, beating Vice President Hubert Humphrey and Alabama Governor George Wallace in the general election.

January 20, 1969 - Nixon is inaugurated as the 37th President of the United States, declaring in his inaugural address, "The greatest honor that history can bestow is the title of peacemaker."

February 1969 - Nixon makes his first foreign trip as president to Europe, visiting France, Great Britain, Belgium, and the Vatican.

July 20, 1969 - Nixon makes the longest long-distance phone call in history, as astronauts Neil Armstrong and Buzz Aldrin take mankind's first steps on the moon.

November 3, 1969 - Nixon receives overwhelming support from the "silent majority" following a televised address announcing his plan to honorably end the Vietnam War.

January 1, 1970 - Nixon signs the National Environmental Policy Act, and launches several environmental initiatives including the Clean Air and Clean Water Acts, the Mammal Marine Protection Act, and the creation of the Environmental Protection Agency.

April 30, 1970 - In a nationally televised address, President Nixon announces military incursion into Cambodia, where communist sanctuaries are aiding the North Vietnamese and Vietcong.

June 12, 1971 - Nixon's daughter Tricia marries Edward Finch Cox in the Rose Garden at the White House.

July 15, 1971 - Nixon announces that he has been invited to China, ending a quarter of a century of hostility in Sino-American relations.

October 12, 1971 - A joint announcement is issued in Washington and Moscow confirming that President Nixon will visit the Soviet Union three months after returning from China.

February 21-28, 1972 - Nixon makes a historic trip to China, meeting with Chairman Mao Tse-Tung and Premier Chou En-Lai, and agreeing on a roadmap to peaceful relations through the Shanghai Communique.

May 21-27, 1972 - Nixon journeys to the Soviet Union and signs the historic agreement on the limitation of strategic arms with Premier Leonid Brezhnev.

June 17, 1972 – Five are arrested in burglary at DNC headquarters at the Watergate Office building.

November 7, 1972 - Nixon is re-elected with largest mandate in American history, winning 49 out 50 states, and nearly 61 percent of the popular vote.

December 18-30, 1972 - "Christmas bombing" of North Vietnam.

January 27, 1973 - Peace treaty ending the Vietnam War is signed in Paris.

June 22, 1973 - Soviet Premier Leonid Brezhnev visits the United States. A Prevention of Nuclear War Agreement is signed.

October 10, 1973 - Vice President Spiro Agnew resigns after corruption charges beginning when he was county executive of Baltimore, Maryland. Gerald Ford becomes vice president the next day.

October 1973 - Nixon provides massive American military aid to Israel during the Yom Kippur War, ensuring its survival.

June 1974 - Nixon re-engages the Middle East as the first president to visit Egypt, Israel, Jordan, Syria, and Saudi Arabia.

June 27-30, 1974 – House Judiciary Committee adopts three articles of impeachment.

July 24, 1974 – Supreme Court rules in U.S. v. Nixon that president Nixon must hand over subpoenaed tapes to John Sirica, U.S. District Court Chief Judge.

August 8, 1974 - Nixon announces his decision to resign as President of the United States and returns as a private citizen to his San Clemente home.

September 8, 1974 – President Gerald Ford pardons Nixon for his role in Watergate scandal.

Summer 1977 - With over 45 million people watching, the Nixon-Frost interview becomes the most-ever watched political interview in history.

1978 - Nixon releases his memoirs, *RN*, which sell more than 300,000 copies, becoming the best selling presidential memoir ever. He will complete a total of ten books before his death.

October 1981 - The Nixons move to Saddle River, New Jersey.

July 19, 1990 - Attends dedication of the Richard Nixon Library and Birthplace with four presidents and their first ladies, and 50,000 friends and supporters.

Summer 1990 - The Nixons move to Park Ridge, New Jersey.

June 22, 1993 - First Lady Pat Nixon dies at home in Park Ridge, New Jersey, at the age of 81 and is laid to rest four days later at the Nixon Library.

January 1994 - On the 25th anniversary of his first inauguration as president, Nixon opens the Nixon Center for Peace and Freedom, a Washington foreign policy think tank based on pragmatic and principled realism.

1994 - Nixon finishes his tenth and final book, *Beyond Peace*, which is published posthumously.

April 22, 1994 - President Nixon dies at 81 in New York City.

April 27, 1994 - Nixon is laid to rest at his birthplace and boyhood home in Yorba Linda, next to First Lady Pat Nixon. Presidents Bush, Reagan, Carter, and Ford attend the funeral, as does then-Senate Minority Leader Bob Dole. Reverend Billy Graham officiates the ceremonies, which tens of millions watch on television.

Figure – 2016 Richard Nixon presidential dollar coin

Acknowledgements

I would like to thank Lisa Zahn and Andreea Mihaela for help in preparation of this book. All the photographs are from the public domain. The quotes at the beginning of each chapter are from Brainyquote.com.

References and Further Reading

Shepard, G. *The Real Watergate Scandal: Collusion, Conspiracy, and the Plot that Brought Nixon Down*. Regnery History. 2015.

Drew, E. *Richard Nixon*. The American Presidents. Times Books. 2007.

Matuz, R. *The Presidents Fact Book: The Achievements, Campaigns, Events, Triumphs, Tragedies, and Legacies of Every President From George Washington to Barack Obama*. Black Dog & Leventhal Publishers, New York. 2009.

Reeves, T.C. *Twentieth-Century America: A Brief History*. Oxford University Press. 2000.

Rorabaugh, W.J. *The Real Making of the President: Kennedy, Nixon, and the 1960 Election*. University Press of Kansas. 2009.

Weiner, T. *One Man Against the World: The Tragedy of Richard Nixon*. Henry Holt and Company, New York. 2015.

About the Author

Doug West is a retired aerospace engineer, small business owner, and experienced non-fiction writer with several books to his credit. His writing interests are general, with expertise in science, history, biographies, numismatics, and "How-to" topics. Doug has a B.S. in Physics from the Missouri School of Science and Technology and a Ph.D. in General Engineering from Oklahoma State University. He lives with his wife and little dog, "Scrappy," near Kansas City, Missouri. Additional books by Doug West can be found at http://www.amazon.com/Doug-West/e/B00961PJ8M. Follow the author on Facebook at https://www.facebook.com/30minutebooks.

Figure – Doug West (photo by Karina Cinnante-West)

Additional Books by Doug West

Buying and Selling Silver Bullion Like a Pro
How to Write, Publish, and Market Your Own Audio Book
A Short Biography of the Scientist Sir Isaac Newton
A Short Biography of the Astronomer Edwin Hubble
Galileo Galilei – A Short Biography
Benjamin Franklin – A Short Biography
The Astronomer Cecilia Payne-Gaposchkin – A Short
Biography
The American Revolutionary War – A Short History
Coinage of the United States – A Short History
John Adams – A Short Biography
In the Footsteps of Columbus (Annotated) Introduction
and Biography Included (with Annie J. Cannon)
Alexander Hamilton – Illustrated and Annotated (with
Charles A. Conant)
Harlow Shapley – Biography of an Astronomer
Alexander Hamilton – A Short Biography
The Great Depression – A Short History
Jesse Owens, Adolf Hitler and the 1936 Summer Olympics
Thomas Jefferson – A Short Biography
Gold of My Father – A Short Tale of Adventure
Making Your Money Grow with Dividend Paying Stocks –
Revised Edition
The French and Indian War – A Short History
The Mathematician John Forbes Nash Jr. – A Short
Biography
The British Prime Minister Margaret Thatcher – A Short
Biography
Vice President Mike Pence – A Short Biography
President Jimmy Carter – A Short Biography
President Ronald Reagan – A Short Biography
President George H. W. Bush – A Short Biography

Dr. Robert H. Goddard – A Brief Biography - Father of American Rocketry and the Space Age

Index

Made in the USA
Lexington, KY
18 November 2019

57251933R00037